MOVING AT THE SPEED OF ME

OLENTHIA R. BOARDLEY

TO: Bishop Marcus:

Thank you for your love, Support & Guidance. You have always be my inspiration as I have watched you grow. Your strength has helped me move forward! and I thank you. *Olenthia R. Boardley*

Published by Olenthia R. Boardley

ISBN:10:1535153024
ISBN-13:978-1535153027

NOV 2016

DEDICATION

This book is dedicated to my mother, Louise P. Longus and my father, Milton W. Longus (deceased), who is watching and smiling at me from Heaven. With my parents' nurturing, support, and guidance, I am who I am today, still moving at the speed of me toward being and giving my best. I want to thank you Mom and Dad as I continue to strive to make you proud of me.

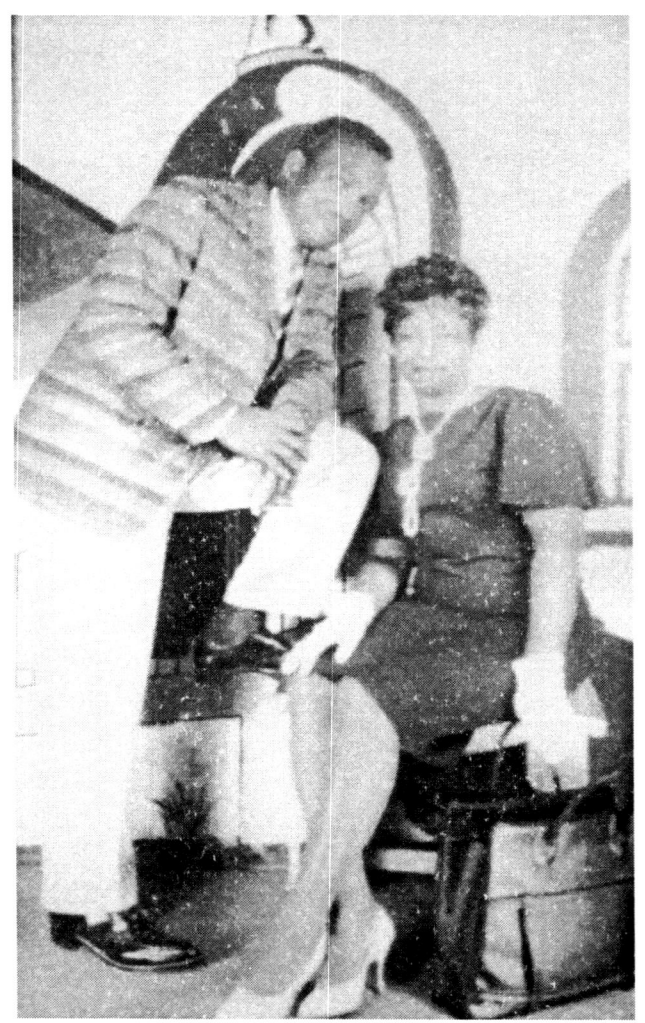

MILTON W. LONGUS & LOUSIE P. LONGUS

TABLE OF CONTENTS

ACKNOWLEDGMENTS

I would like to acknowledge the following individuals for their support, love, mentorship, encouragement, and guidance. Grace Bradford, former choir director, Woodson Jr. High School, and Asbury United Methodist Church Youth Choir. Bishop Marcus Mathews, Baltimore Washington Conference. Shelby Tuck Horton, Master Bridal Consultant, State Manager for MDDC Chapter, The Association of Bridal Consultants, and Life Coach; The Association of Bridal Consultants Corporate Office. Dr. Willie Jolley, Award-winning speaker, singer, best-selling author, and media personality; Reverend Dr. Ianther Mills, Senior Pastor, Asbury United Methodist Church; Tina L. Greer, Business Growth Strategist, speaker, and author; Cheryl Wood, Award-winning international speaker, author, coach and entrepreneur; William T. Spencer, digital artist, Douglas E. Gibbs, graphic restoration artist, Back cover photo by Lisa Feet, of Lisa Feet Photography. I would also like to thank my friends and family members. A very special acknowledgment to my children, Jenell D. Boardley and Jason M. H. Boardley. I am so very proud of you both. To my husband, Ronald D. Boardley, who I admire and respect, you are my rock, my support system, my love, my all.

MOVING AT THE SPEED OF ME

INTRODUCTION

My journey of moving at the speed of me is a journey of life, lessons, and perseverance. My short stories give you a glimpse of family, mentors, and business influences in my life. Your life's journey molds and shapes you. However, there will come a time when you will make a decision to stay or move out of your comfort zone. Sometimes we become complacent and stay where we are because it's familiar and we settle for not moving forward. We settle for average. We are not average; we all have gifts inside us. You have to find a way to express your gifts, though you live in public housing, a shelter, or in a home as a single parent. It does not matter your station in life. You have to find the strength to understand and be determined to move forward because you know you have a gift you want to share. What if you are not moving at the speed of friends and family? What if you have to do something over twice, maybe four times, until you get it right? The accomplishment is getting it done at your speed. But don't sit back now. Keep moving, keep digging, put on your blinders; it may be the only way you can move forward. Sometimes you will have to move some family and friends out of the way to obtain your journey's passion. Don't let anyone tell you that you can't do something. When faced with adversity from family and friends, find the strength to move past them and move forward. Use this book to inspire yourself, to give you confidence, to give you energy, to let you know that the constant tugging and pulling on your heart are your gifts trying to get out. Inside your being, you can feel the pull of wanting to start a business, to become an entrepreneur. Just know it is possible. Use the tips in this book as a starting point to begin your journey when researching your business. Share my book with business colleagues, friends, and family members and connect with me on social media. My gifts are sharable in writing or in person. I would love to come and talk with you or your group about starting your own business. Passing on knowledge is the most important thing we can do to educate those who would follow in our footsteps. If I can encourage or uplift just one person, that would be my greatest joy. My journey is far from over. My journey continues from the little girl who grew up in public housing and liked to put events together, to owning my own events business. Now I am pushing myself again as I write this book, rebrand my business, and continue to educate myself to be the best me I can be. This will help me share my gifts with all of you, which is my joy. Just know I will continue to move at the speed of me, but I will always get the job done!

CHAPTER 1

A GENTLE GIANT

When you are the fifth child in a group of seven your life can be a bit hectic. As early as I can remember, I was the little one though I had two younger brothers. My mom stayed home and took care of all of us while my father, the breadwinner, went out to work each day. He seemed so big and tall. When he talked, the room shook. Dad's footsteps were loud and hard; the room vibrated. When dad came home from work, all the children would scamper and get out of his way. My dad commanded order, quiet, and food. My mother provided a good household and great meals. We were fed, clean, had a warm safe environment to live in, and we always had fun. She made our home fun, from cleaning our rooms to playing dodge ball in the back yard. Although we lived in public housing, I had no idea that we were considered poor. We lived in a house, we had plenty to eat, and did not want for anything. I had no idea what a struggle it was to feed all seven of us. I had no idea that my dad had a full time job, a part time job, and some odd jobs on the weekend to keep us warm and fed; thus the absentness. I remember my Dad not being home a lot, which sometimes made me feel sad. I would not see him for days at a time. He would leave very early in the morning before I got up, and come home very late in the evening after mom had put us to bed. So, as a little child maybe seven years of age, I started to get up early in the morning before he left for work and would have a morning cup of coffee with him. Yes, that's right—coffee. My mother would get up at 4:00 in the morning to prepare breakfast for my dad as well as lunch to take with him to work. We had a percolator for brewing coffee. You could smell the brewing coffee all over the house starting at 4:00 am. My mother would start making bacon, eggs, and toast. I would be lying in bed smelling all those aromas that give you a warm feeling inside. We knew she was up preparing things for dad, but we also knew that we should not come down the stairs, for this was mom and dad's quiet time. This was their time without children when they talked about family issues, housing matters, what kid needed to go in to see a doctor, and other family matters. Someone always had a cold, was sick, or cut some part of their bodies from having just a little too much fun outside. Mom tried her best to keep us well so that the rest of us would not get sick and have to be taken to see the doctor.

On one very quiet morning when I lay in my bed awake, I did not hear them talking. It was extremely quiet. I worried at first that something was wrong. So, I decided to sneak down the stairs and look through the banister to see what was going on. What I saw was dad drinking his coffee very slowly as if it tasted so good. He was looking at his cup while he drank and appeared to be thinking about something that made him smile and then laugh. I did not see mom anywhere around. Right when I was about to creep myself back up the stairs he spotted me. Oh my goodness! I was frozen in my tracks. I was scared to death as he peered at me with those very light brown almost hazel eyes as if he was going to eat me up. (Which was one of his sayings he would tell us kids if we got out of line–that he would "eat us up alive!") I was about to start crying because I knew I was in trouble and I was going to get a whipping. All of a sudden, instead of a stern look, a big smile came over his face and he motioned me to come to him. I slowly stood up and walked off the steps toward him. He motioned me to sit on his lap. Instead of being scolded, he asked me in a soft voice, "What are you doing up this early?" I was shocked; this was new for me for I was accustomed to this big booming voice, this very tall man towering over everyone, and the ground shaking as he walked by. Who was this person? Was this my dad? I did not know he could be like this. So with fear still in my voice I said, "I got up early so I could see you. I have not seen you in days." Again, I thought he was going to be mad and yell at me. Instead, he put his arms around me, squeezed me tight, and gave me a big kiss on my cheek. He said he was sorry that I missed him. He explained as well as he could to a seven-year-old that grown people have to work every day. By doing so, he could provide us with food, shelter, and clothes. I remember thinking it must be a lot of work to do all that. I now had an understanding of why I did not see him as much. We sat and talked for a little longer before he said he had to get going to work. I asked him one final question. "Hey dad what is that you are drinking?" He said coffee. I asked if I could have some because he made it look like it tastes so good. Dad said, "I will let you have a sip, but you can't tell mom." I took a little sip. It was black and bitter. I thought the taste of the coffee would be sweet because of the big smile on his face. I determined that I really did not like how it tastes. That did not matter because I was having special time with dad. I pretended that the coffee tasted good thus starting a morning ritual with my dad. On some mornings when I got up, I would see him and we would have a little talk and some coffee; other times he would be gone already, but he would leave a little sip of coffee in his cup on the table for me. Needless to say, my other siblings got wise to what was going on with the coffee in the cup on the table. This turned into whoever got up the earliest or the first one down the stairs would be the one who would get to sip the last bit of coffee dad left in his cup. "The early bird gets the worm" is a true phrase in our household. Seven children; I have six siblings. Imagine this for a moment; each one of us having different personalities and characteristics.

My siblings consist of four brothers—two older and two younger, and two sisters who are older than I am. One of my first memories growing up was sitting around the dining table as a family having dinner. As I looked around the dining room table, I would see siblings who looked something like me, and some I think, didn't look like me at all. My oldest brother is tall, dark, and handsome like my father, with very bright eyes and beautiful white teeth. He is also the family clown, always playing jokes on everyone. He would make us so angry because his jokes where not always funny to us. To annoy most of the siblings, he would do the un-thinkable and steal, hide, or eat the food off your plate.

As I said, his jokes were not always funny. Mealtime was taken very seriously in our household. Imagine this—you have been playing all day, ripping and running all over the neighborhood, and now it is time for dinner. You go and wait in line to get in the bathroom to wash up and prepare for dinner. One person at a time, following the routine of washing our hands, sitting in our seat at the table, and bowing our heads to say grace. Our prayer was, "God is grace and God is good, and we thank him for our food. By Gods hands we all are fed; give us Lord our daily bread, AMEN!" While saying grace you could smell the aroma of the biscuits mom had prepared for us from scratch. I could not wait to sink my teeth into the soft warm dough. When I opened my eyes, I noticed my biscuit was gone! I looked to the right and then to the left, and just when I was about to call for mother, my oldest brother smiled real big and put my biscuit back on my plate. When I was ready to sink my teeth into my biscuit, I noticed a bite had already been taken out of it. When I looked at my brother, he would look away as if he had done nothing. This was one of his many jokes we were all subjected to. I might add, we were not amused!

However, on an inspiring note, my big brother was very smart. He truly excelled in school. This was great for him, but hard for us. When one large family attends the same schools in the neighborhood, elementary, middle and high school, and you have older siblings ahead of you, well let's just say the teachers remember the ones ahead of you. Therefore, we would always be compared to our older brother. He was an outstanding student, so the expectation and the reputation to live up to was and could be very hard to follow. So mountains to climb were already set for us and we had to climb and conquer the best we could. My second oldest brother was taller than my oldest brother. He has beautiful light eyes and is very fair in complexion. I remember how he used to run all the time all over the neighborhood. So much so, that he was given the nickname rabbit. He was very fast and would always challenge other kids in the neighborhood in races. Most of the time he would win the race. One day he received a new pair of tennis shoes. Well, he thought he could fly. My mother thought he would wear those new tennis shoes out in one day from all the races that he participated in. When he did not win a race, he would keep challenging you until he beat you. Although he was tall, he was not muscular, so he would do everything he could to build muscles. He tried all types of workouts, mixing of power drinks, and lifting weights. He transformed himself. He actually bulked up. I remember how proud he was of his progress. So much so, that he tried out for our neighborhood recreation center basketball team. He made the team and all that running paid off, for he was quick up and down the court. He went on to play in high school and excelled to become one of the star players. It was amazing watching him persevere through pushing himself forward. Even when his friend discouraged him, telling him he was too small and would not get bigger, but he did not let that stop him. He used that negative feedback to push himself forward. He showed them, and reached his goal. Wow, what a testament!

My eldest sister is the mother figure. I remember from an early age, if we needed something, we would ask my eldest sister before we would ask mom. It was like a test. She could tell us if what we wanted would pass mom. Most of the time she would tell us not to ask mom something or it might get us into trouble. It was as if she knew the mood of our mother and when it was a good time or a bad time to ask a question. My eldest sister is a beautiful person with a gorgeous complexion. Her skin is a creamy almond brown and everyone always notices how beautiful she is. Like the second mommy in the household, she would always help with the chores. Our house was so clean that you would never know that seven children lived there. I remember my oldest sister sweeping the floor. You can image there was plenty of spillage with a bunch of kids. She would clean and sweep all the floors to the point where they would shine. My mother gave her a crate to stand on at the sink in the kitchen to wash the dishes. It looked like fun to me at the time, but I realized later that it was not something she liked to do. My oldest sister also excelled in school and could keep up. She followed in the footsteps of our oldest brother. She took the time to help us little ones with homework and made sure our assignments where completed. She would also help us prepare when we had a spelling test. Spelling tests seem to be the ultimate exam to be completed. I remember pulling out my little green lined paper with my spelling words on it. We would begin the drill with, "Say the word, use the word in a sentence, and spell the word." Then for homework we would have to take a clean sheet of green or white lined paper and write each word five or ten times and turn that in to our teacher. My printing was so big; I would use up several sheets of paper. My sister would show me how to hold the pencil to help me write smaller. It would seem we would work on this for hours. With her help, I learned to write smaller and neater too. She was very patient with me, always encouraging me to slow down and focus. She let me know I could do better if I just put my best efforts forward. As an older sister, she always found the time to help and encourage any sibling who needed that extra push and love, even with her busy schedule. I watched her grow into an outstanding teenager and later an advocate for her community. Wanting to learn more about how to leverage the growth of her community with various projects, she worked full time, raised her family, and went back to school. Though this was very challenging, with the help of her husband she was able to complete her graduate degree. She opened her own business in her community to build brighter futures for the residents by assisting underprivileged families acquire their first homes or apartment housing. With that giving spirit, she continues to work on programs to encourage, motivate, and uplift her neighborhood.

I have another sister who is shorter in height than me, but is eleven months older than me. She is the one who looks most like our father, from the structure of her face and nose to the color of her eyes, almost hazel. We wondered where all this eye color came from? We found out that my grandmother, my father's mother was a Cherokee Indian. She was the one with these qualities; slender nose, high cheekbones and very light eyes. I wish I would have had the opportunity to meet her, but she passed before I was born. This second eldest sister was the one who was the most independent one. Whenever she had a hard time learning how to do anything she would just do it over and over until she learned how to do it correctly. She would get frustrated, but she would not let her fears or anxiety slow her down. She was determined to get it done. My sister realized that she had a problem with words and placement. She practiced hard with spelling words then learned how to dissect sentences. This became a game of who could complete an assignment first. She learned to identify every part of a sentence to include: noun, pronoun, verb, and dangling participle.

This was known then as a game of hangman, which she won over and over again. This evolved into making her an excellent writer and very good with subject matter of English in school. She used these skills to acquire a job as a secretary and program manager. Her part time job in high school turned into a full time job upon graduation. My sister did the unthinkable when she was barely eighteen years old. She moved out of the house into her own apartment. I was so afraid for her. I thought she was too young. She had other ideas, and she wanted her own independence. I was so proud of how she did not let her fears hold her back. She knew what she wanted and went after it. Yes, life is scary but she challenged herself, walked in, and conquered her fears, never staying down, always brushing herself off, and moving forward. She continues to do that today. Her perseverance is unstoppable.

I have two younger brothers who have been taller and larger than me since they were ten years old. This put me at a disadvantage. We were called "The Three Little Ones." We were treated much different from the older siblings. From clothes to seating arrangements at the table, we were displayed for all to see the cute "Three Little Ones" Everyone always thought I was the youngest because I was the smallest. Then being the girl of the final group put me at another disadvantage. My brother, who is eleven months younger than I am, is the artistic one of the family. From an early age, he was always doodling. As he got older, he began to draw by hand large pictures and then painting them. His drawings turned into a collection of paintings. He had an opportunity to display his paintings at several showings. He did very well and received a continual repeat of follow-ups from clients that lead to additional opportunities. We thought this would be the direction he was going to explore further as a career. However, to our surprise, he changed directions and formed his own singing group and disc jockey production company. The group sang around the Washington, D.C., area at various venues, park settings, and churches. His production company would provide music and karaoke events around the city for various venues as well. I watch him grow his passion of art and music. He is truly in his element when he is behind the control board of his music or behind the microphone singing to his guests. His passion has a purpose of bringing music and enjoyment to as many people as he can.

The actual baby of the siblings was the one who was picked on the most, just because he was the last one. He was the quiet one. He did not say much in the beginning. To be honest with all the noise going on from six other siblings, he may have felt like there was enough noise in the house and he would not be heard. We continued to invite him in and told him to speak up and soon he changed and became very vocal. My youngest brother was always in the kitchen watching mom as she prepared the meals. My mother began to let him help with a few preparations of meals. He would stir and mix corn meal for the corn muffins, and the batter for Sunday cake. This was a real treat because you could lick the bowl and spoons as part of clean up. How many of you remember that as a kid? My youngest brother loved being in the kitchen cooking. My mother soon let him assist with other cooking projects under her supervision. As he got older, he began to make breakfast for us. He made excellent pancakes and scramble eggs. He did so well at cooking, my brothers would ask him to cook for them when mom was not home. As he got older he applied for and was hired at jobs that would allow him to cook. He has worked in several locations throughout the D.C. metropolitan area as a Master Chef. Although he has had no formal training, he knows everything about food preparation in a large kitchen from cooking and plating to serving the food. He continues as a Master Chef and still dreams of one day having his own restaurant.

My siblings have shown me that you have to go through challenges in life to get to where you truly want to be. Just watching each of them was a building block for me, which let me know that it's okay to work toward your passion at your own speed. Take your time, slow down, and your rewards will come.

"ME AND MY SIBLINGS"

CHAPTER 2

GIVING BACK

As a youth growing up in the inner city, our recreation center was our lifeline. The recreation center and staff would take us on summer bus trips throughout the city. These trips would consist of going to places in the Washington, D.C., area such as the National Zoo, Washington monuments, movies and live theater productions, and the National and Werner Theater. Do you know what happens when you live in a popular city? You never visit the places people travel from long distances to see and its right in your back yard. Of all the field trips we went on, live theater was what held my attention the most. Lights, camera, action, and live music; I could see myself singing, dancing, and acting in the show. As a young child, and well into my young adult years, the arts and theater have had a major influence on my life. From my first vocal music class in classical, jazz, and gospel, to dance classes in ballet, jazz, and tap, I tried to do it all. From my inner city training, I was able to perform in theatrical productions from the "Summer in The Parks Program," theater programs with my church, and dance recitals. As I learned, i gave back to my community. I was hired as a roving instructor and taught dance classes in recreation centers throughout

Washington, D.C. Some of the students from the recreation centers where inspired to go further with their training. This made me feel on top of the world to help kids in my own area that I grew up in. During this time, I was allowed to take some of my students on field trips to their first live theater productions. I could see their faces light up with every aspect of the trip. I could see me in them when I was their age. Having this experience for the first time, I knew they would never forget it!

I began, at that time, talking with kids and letting them know "it does not matter where you are now; it's where you are going in the future." I must say that some of them did feel stuck, and feeling they could not do any better. I explained to them where I grew up and that I too was an inner city kid just like them. They were surprised because they thought I could not understand their struggle. Once they understood that I too grew up in the inner city, they could relate. By telling my story, they blossomed in every way which improved their outlook on life that all things are possible if you just work at it. In addition to the weekly talks, at the end of each six-week dance session we would put on a full production with costumes and make-up. And then it was lights, camera, action—it was show time. This made them remember the live production we had seen. The students imagined themselves on the stage of the

National and Warner Theater. From participating in the recreation center productions, some of students who were very shy and reserved came out of their shells and soared. Some of the students were loud, rough around the edges, and had a discipline problem. As a result of being part of the program, they began to learn how to follow instructions and be team players instead of causing problems and acting out; starving for attention. When the productions were over and they received standing ovations, and certificates of completion, they were excited, emotional, and thrilled beyond belief. They did it! They conquered their fear, went out of their comfort zone, put their best foot forward, and could not believe the results they did all on their own by doing the work. I was so proud of them. They were so proud of themselves and their family and love ones where totally shocked at what could be accomplished in a short six-week session. I could see on my students' faces that they too had been transformed and changed. The power of knowing I contributed to the change was the best feeling ever. As my mother would say, "It's time to make a change. It's not going to be easy, but it must be done." When my youngest brother was about eight years old, my mother went to work for the federal government. This was an adjustment, but the older children stepped up and filled in the gaps (as well as they could). This gave my mother the opportunity to develop herself outside of the home. It was a chance for her to explore what she wanted to do to educate herself and make a contribution to her work environment. This was very new for my mother. She was out of her comfort zone, but she was going to embrace this new adventure full steam ahead. She fully enjoyed the opportunity to discover a new side of herself and come into her own; not that of mother or wife. After twenty years of service at her place of employment and the passing of my father, my mother retired. I decided to do something very special for her to show my appreciation for all her work and the sacrifices she had made for the family. I put together a package titled "Queen for a Day." The package included Limo transportation all day, a special breakfast, spa package, hair, nails, shopping spree, gifts, and a surprise dinner with friends and family members in attendance. She was so excited and was truly surprised as the day of events unfolded. She laughed and cried the entire day and has been talking about this experience ever since, as if it just happened yesterday. From that event my business was born— "The Royal Treatment." I received several requests to assist in managing various types of events for individuals. My former training from childhood, organizing small events for friends and family provided the initial skills needed in order to direct and manage my events. I used those skills as well as my skills from teaching to help me launch my event planning business.

I have discovered that I like to teach. I have been afforded the opportunity to teach and mentor others who desire to learn how to become event planners. My best reward is passing on knowledge and watching someone else learn and grow from it. The best legacy in life is to share your knowledge for the improvement of others. Knowledge should be released and shared. What you know is a wonderful and powerful concept. Your light will not be diminished because you are you; there is no other person like you. The planet will evolve better if you do your part and help others. Don't ever think that you know it all. You must always be in the mind set to be teachable. I found that what I have in my head and heart is knowledge, and that I can pass it on to others. I surprised myself when I told part of my story and how just that small glimpse of who I am helped someone to release their fears and be encouraged to move forward. I was surprised to find my information had value. I challenge each of you reading this book to tell your story. Try it, you might surprise yourself and be amazed of the reactions you receive for others. What you know today is enough and can truly help someone.

CHAPTER 3

QUEEN FOR A DAY

My mother can be described by the word and definition of mother, which is: "A woman in relation to a child or children to whom she has given birth; a female parent, a women of authority a protector, disciplinarian and friend." A mother is a selfless, loving human who must sacrifice many of her wants and needs for the wants and needs of the children. A mother works hard to make sure her child or children are equipped with the knowledge, skills, and abilities to become a competent human being. Being a mother is perhaps the hardest, most rewarding job a woman will ever experience.

My mother grew up with four siblings—three sisters and one brother. From an early age, her childhood was a struggle, but they had love in the family. One of my favorite stories my mother told us was that as a young child she would get up, and go out after her chores and (hustle). My mother would always say, "If you really want something it's not just going to be easy and just appear you have to work for it." So, at an early age as she calls it, "she got her hustle on." She did this by collecting and selling bottles. She would take her large pouch and walk around her neighborhood looking for bottles. This was during the time you could get money for turning in bottles. After hours of searching and collecting bottles, she would take them to the local grocery store in the area. She knew that she could receive anywhere from two to five cents for each bottle and would often have to negotiate with the owner to get what her bottles were worth. She was a shrewd business girl because if the owner tried to give her a lesser amount then she would tell him that she would have to take her business to the next grocery store. This would have been a very difficult feat because it was quite a distance away and she was not riding a bike or anything; she was on foot. Besides, she had a certain time she would have be back home for evening chores and to help with the preparation of supper. She managed to stick to her guns and was able to get the asking price for her bottles. She would bring home her money and show her mother how enterprising she was with her little business and her mother was pleased. Unfortunately, her mother would also take most of her money and use it for the household. Mom thought it should be hers since she worked so hard to get it. She learned at an early age about saving and the management of money. She continued with her little hustle of collecting bottles and anything else that she could find which could be bartered or sold for money. She would continue to give the money to her mother but she only gave her half of what she made and saved the rest for herself. She used her money to buy a new pair of socks. This was very important for she walked all over the neighborhood and to school, which was quite a distance. Mother told me that this was the best lesson ever at an early age about the management of money. She used this acquired skill of money management once she got married and began to have children. With one salary in the household, she had to find ways to stretch every penny. I remember it always seemed as if my Mom never stopped cooking, cleaning, and washing clothes. My mother was always in perpetual motion. It was sort of like a dance, going from one room to the next until everything was finished. Also, while doing this dance my mother would sing. What a beautiful voice! She said it made the cleaning of the house and chores go faster. I really enjoyed the music when she would sing jazz. She would sing along with the music from the little turntable we had. One day we came home from school, did our schoolwork, and then had dinner like usual, but this time after dinner we had a family meeting. The air was thick. Mom looked very serious and dad looked as if he was upset about something. I felt uneasy and I felt like I wanted to cry. Mother began by saying that she was very proud of all of us. She said that we were doing very well in school and to keep up the great work. She then began to ask us all questions about our morning and evening schedule. It was as if we were rehearsing for a play. She would say, "When you get up in the morning what do you do first?" Then she asked about what we did second, and so on. We would all answer in unison without missing a beat. Then she continued, "In the evenings what is the most important thing to complete when you come in?" Again, in unison we would say homework. She would say that we were big children and that we could take care of ourselves. With that, I began to cry. I asked where she was going. "We need you here with us to take care of us!" It felt like goodbye. I thought," Why? Why is she leaving us?" So I asked again, "Are you going to leave us?"

She replied, "Yes, I am leaving." I felt like I could not breathe. Just as I began to cry, she then said, "Yes, I am leaving. I start work next week. I have decided to go back to work." The room exploded with all sorts of questions. She turned and looked at my father and said, "We decided that it's time for me to go back to work to help with the finances of the household." I could tell by looking at my father that he did not like that statement and was not fully onboard, nor did he agree. You see, my dad was from the era where the man took care of the family financially by going to work outside the home, and the women-folk stayed home and took care of the family. He must have felt a little embarrassed at first, but later he came to realize that it was a good thing for the entire household because we could now afford a few more things such as clothing, food, and household items for our large growing family. My mother worked for 27 years until her retirement.

I had this great idea regarding mom's retirement. I coined it "Queen for a Day" it would become the cornerstone for my event business. I pitched all the details to my siblings and they were on board. This was going to be a complete surprise for her. As I got to work putting everything together, I was so excited to do this knowing that my mother, the Queen of the family, was so well deserving of anything that would bring a smile to her face. I had hoped that this celebration would help relieve the pain of being a widow, for the gentle giant, my father had passed away four years earlier. As the time came near, I informed her sisters at the last minute. I know that they should have been told earlier, but it was going to be a surprise. They have an interesting habit of letting the fun slip out because they get so excited before an event, so I took no chances. I called each aunt and give them some of the information about the plans for the day and their part of the planned surprise regarding what they needed to do. I was afraid that when I spoke with them, I would get chewed out. So as I dialed the numbers, my heart started to pound faster and my forehead began to perspire. After I finished talking with them, they were all delighted and wanted to know more about the details. I did not give them all the details. The fun would be for my mom to be surrounded by her friends and family and tell her story with all the eyes on her as she recanted the excitement of her "Royal Treatment" day. Her sisters were all on board now and promised not to spill the beans. They only had one day to hold their excitement. It was time for lights, camera, action! Mom's Queen for a Day event started with a limousine dispatched to her home that she could use all day while making her scheduled appointments. I told her I would arrive at her house to pick her up and then bring her to my house for breakfast. Instead, I sent a limousine. I called her and told her I was outside waiting to take her to my house. When she opened the door, she saw a big black shiny limousine, red carpet rolled out for her to walk on, and Mr. Charles, the driver waiting for her. I knew she would not get in so I called her back. "Mother, this car is for you. I had so much to do in preparation for breakfast I thought I would send a limousine instead. Enjoy the ride and I will see you when you get here. Mr. Charles, the driver, will take care of you. As she came back to the door and began to lock it, Mr. Charles got out of his car and assisted her down the stairs as the red carpet he had previously rolled out for her awaited the Queens entrance to the limousine. Mr. Charles opened the passenger side door and helped mother into the limousine. By this time all of the neighbors came out to see who the big black limousine was for? When they saw it was for my mother they cheered her on! This made her really feel like a Queen, and it was just the beginning of her Queen for a Day experience. Before leaving, Mr. Charles gave my mother a small box and an envelope and instructed her to open the small box first and the envelope second. She opened the small box very carefully. My mom did not want to mess up the wrapping paper because it was so pretty. Inside the box was a small crystal ornament. Then she opened the envelope. It was a note from me. It read, "Sit back and relax while you enjoy being treated like a Queen for the Day." Then the driver handed her a chilled orange juice and the phone and begin to drive off to come to my house. I called her in the car while she was in route, just to check on her. I could not understand a word she was saying because she was crying.

Once she got herself together, she just kept saying, "Thank you, thank you, thank you." Then she stopped crying long enough to ask a lot of questions and especially about what was next. I told her we were going to have breakfast, and that I would see her soon. Once she arrived, the driver rolled out the red carpet again, and then opened the passenger door.

My daughter, who was quite small at the time, greeted

her with flowers and escorted her into the house. You know how grandmothers are with grandchildren; she began to cry again. My daughter asked, "Grandmother, are you okay?"

She replied, "Yes, I am just so happy. These are happy tears." Mom had a wonderful meal with my husband, my young son and daughter, and me. She marveled at the dishes, the good china, and commented on the teacups. She enjoyed the meal and visiting with her grandchildren.

My daughter then announced, "Well, Grandmother, it's time for you to go!" My mother looked surprised because she did not know where she was going. We walked her to the front door and explained to her that she was going to her next stop, compliments of the Queen for a Day experience. She was shocked and amazed to see the limousine still parked in front of my house. She wanted to know why the limousine was still there. We explained to her that the limousine was hers for the day and that Mr. Charles would be escorting her to her next appointment. Well, she did not know what that was. We escorted her to the limousine and the driver was ready with the red carpet and standing outside the limousine, holding the door for her entrance. After she got in the car, I handed her an envelope and the driver gave her a small box and a chilled glass of pineapple drink. The note said, "Sit back and relax. You are now off to your next appointment." Inside the box was a note. The note said, "You will truly want to wear this now." It was a decorative scarf. As the limousine pulled away, I called her on the phone. I then explained, that she was being treated as "Queen for the day" with several stops along the way before going back home. She was overjoyed and tears were flowing everywhere. Her next stop was the Spa where she was treated to a pedicure, manicure, and eyebrow trimming. She loved it; so much so that after this event she treated herself several more times. With the completion of her Spa appointment, she was driven to a women's clothing store located at the mall. The note that the driver gave her told her where to go and who to ask for. Once she stepped out of the car she was greeted by the manager, who ushered her in to her own private room. They offered her tea and cookies. They asked her to relax and enjoy the show they had prepared especially for her. She was treated to a fashion show of several items that I pre-packed for her. Upon the end of the show she was asked to pick the one outfit that she liked the best. The item was wrapped and sent with her when she left the store. The limo sitting outside the store waiting for her caused a commotion. Everyone wanted to know who the passenger was. When my mother came out of the store and the driver sprang into action everyone stopped, watched, and made comments about who they thought she was. Yes, she said she felt like a Queen with all the special attention she was getting. On to the next stop, the driver stated to mom, "We are in route back to your house." I called her in the car to find out how she was enjoying her day thus far. Again, tears of joy and lots of "thank you, thank you!" She thought her Queen for a Day experience was over but it was not.

Once she arrived at home, mother was given another envelope. It read, "You have time to relax and refresh for two hours. Please dress in the outfit placed on your bed. Your driver will be back in two and one half hours to pick you up. Be ready for dinner." Once again, the driver sprang into action, returned at the assigned time, and drove mother to a local dinner theater where all her children and their families, additional family members, and most of her church family greeted her. She was overjoyed beyond her expectations; she truly lost it as she received hugs and kisses from everyone. During dinner, the master of ceremony for the dinner theater did a special presentation about my mother, announcing her name, and asking her to stand and be recognized. As she stood, the spotlight shined on her while everyone acknowledged her with a standing ovation and a round of applause. She felt so much joy, excitement, and appreciation. She was truly humbled by this experience.

She wanted to go back outside to see the driver before he left and she gave Mr. Charles a hug and kiss and expressed her thanks for all that he did for her Queen for a Day adventure. After her Queen for a Day event, family and church family members who did not attend her special event heard about all that happened to her during the day. She received additional congratulations, hugs, and kisses for weeks following her special day. She has told this story over and over many times with delight.

My mother, like all mothers, sacrifice and give of themselves, placing their needs, wants, and desires on hold, putting themselves last and not expecting anything in return. Your mother is a Queen! Every mother deserves to be treated like a Queen every day! I want you to plan a special day for your mother or that very special woman in your life and give her a very special "Queen for a Day" moment!

CHAPTER 4

THE ROYAL TREATMENT

The "Queen for a Day" experience blossomed into my business today, which focuses on the royal treatment.

The Royal Treatment is my desire and vision to treat everyone to exquisite elegant events in a Royal way. The Royal Treatment would consist of assisting my clients with planning and executing pivotal business, special events, and celebrations. Now on the move, I was officially open for business. Friends and family members who attended my signature event, "Queen for a Day," began to recommend me to other individuals and other small businesses to assist with their events, launches, and open houses. I was very green with running a business and did not know how much time to put in, how to charge for services, and how to say no and mean it, and receive what I am worth. I began to do weddings and discovered that I truly had a passion for them. Weddings became the anchor for my small business, as I continued to do other small events as well. The business name was changed to Orbs Royal Treatment because I still wanted to give my clients the Queen and King Royal experience for their weddings. One of their most important days in their life should be loving, exquisite, and royal.   I began to research organizations to help guide me with the professional way to develop and grow my business. Upon review of several companies, I decided to collaborate with The Association of Bridal Consultants, (ABC) ABC Headquarters in Connecticut, President David M. Wood, III.   The Association of Bridal Consultants is the oldest and largest training organization for wedding professionals in the world. ABC currently has over 4,000 members located in all 50 states and in 27 countries. Since 1955, their goals have been to raise professional standards in the wedding industry and to make brides happy. These goals have helped ABC members stand out for their high standards and thereby prosper along the way. I completed the application and within two months received a letter of congratulations and acceptance from the then president and founder of The Association of Bridal Consultants, Mr. Jerry Monaghan. I was surprised and shocked because I received a personnel phone call from Mr. Monaghan. I remember his very deep and regal voice on the other end of the phone. He asked, "Is this Olenthia? Olenthia Boardley?" I was stunned. I said yes, reluctantly, and then he said that he was Jerry Monaghan, President of the Association of Bridal Consultants. I felt so special, I felt like I was speaking to someone presidential. Well, he was actually the president of ABC. He welcomed me to the Association and explained the programs that ABC offers. He asked me why I chose ABC and what I hoped to gain from joining their Association. I explained to him how I started my business and my thirst to learn more and become the best I can be in the event industry. He then told me who my State Manager for my area, Maryland, would be. The State Manager would also be able to answer and address any additional questions or concerns that I might have about ABC. I was assigned to Mrs. Shelby Tuck-Horton, Master Bridal Consultant, State Manager for the Maryland and Washington Chapter. Mrs. Tuck-Horton has become my mentor and friend. With her guidance and support, I was able to meet other like-minded event planners, participate in educational events for event planners, attend quarterly meetings, local area network meetings, and annual corporate meetings held throughout the United States and the Caribbean, and so much more!

Orbs Royal Treatment, LLC is a Business and Special Events company. Since 1997, Orbs Royal Treatment, LLC has been registered with The Association of Bridal Consultants (ABC). It is imperative that you partner yourself with like-minded individuals and associations that can help guide and grow your business. ABC has been paramount in this aspect for helping me grow my business. I have learned everything from the first meeting of a client, service billing for your skills and abilities, and getting the wedding couple down the aisle. I would like to reflect on one of my first weddings prior to joining the Association of Bridal Consultants. Upon meeting with the couple, we agreed on the service fee for Orbs Royal Treatment, LLC to assist with their wedding. My contract was completed; however, the couple would ask me to do more than what we agreed upon. I did not have staff or an assistant so I did everything. After a long and demanding event, I took away a lot of knowledge about what not to do for the next one. Upon joining ABC, I was taught during the interview how to determine and qualify my potential new client as well as how to build my contract for submission or approval and retainer payment. As you know, there are many details to planning and executing events. Although weddings are the anchor of the business, we have also designed the layout of venues for business, church, and social events. The vacations aspect of the company grew out of being asked to do honeymoons for my wedding couples. Upon designing the wedding, the question would always come up, "Where are you going for your honeymoon?" I would then immediately begin researching and arranging for their vacation. After the wedding and honeymoon was completed, I would send my clients a follow-up questionnaire about how they enjoyed our service for their wedding and honeymoon. One of our statements would be, "Please recommend us to your friends and family members." The survey would come back asking if we could book summer and/or weekend trips for them and additional family members. This was great and it was determined that we needed to acquire more education and skill on booking travel. So, I partnered Orbs Royal Treatment with an accredited International Air Transportation Association, IATA, travel agency. Under this program, I received training and became a certified Airlines Reporting Corporation, ARC, Cruise Lines International Association, CLIA member. Doing so allowed me to book travel, reserve airline seats, as well as book cruise trips for my clients. This aspect of the business was very exciting and we were doing a sizeable amount of business. Another lesson learned was that I did not have a proper system in place to handle all the del determined that we would concentrate on business, special events, and honeymoons. Following the process of weddings, you must have a system in place in order to have a proper workflow. The process of accepting an assignment is very detailed and you must be able to convey that process to your clients. Your clients must sign off on that process after they have read and understand all the procedures before any retainer payment is made. The satisfaction of having someone do your bookings for you relieves stress and you have the ease of knowing everything is in place for a wonderful experience. All the client should have to do is pay, pick up the tickets, and go! We also provide services as a travel agent, showing you the best deals and providing a live report of a location we have visited; therefore, giving you a better recommendation with firsthand experience. Remember, at the beginning of 1997 individuals were not as perceptive as they are now with using the internet. Now things have dramatically changed due to the improvement and ease of using the internet. Because of this, I have pulled back from doing full travel services and concentrate more toward honeymoons and group travel. I have now collaborated with Sandals. Sandals's is the family-owned Sandals Resorts International (SRI). Sandals has transformed itself from one brand and one resort in Montego Bay, Jamaica to become one of the most well-known and award-winning hospitality companies in the world. With five brands and twenty-four properties in seven countries including Antigua, The Bahamas, Grenada, Barbados, Jamaica, Saint Lucia, and Turks and Caicos, Sandals Resorts International is the undisputed leader of Caribbean vacation experiences. Sandals remains fiercely committed to the region, dedicating itself to innovative resort development that in the words of Chairman and Founder Gordon "Butch" Stewart, "exceed expectations" for guests, associates, and the people who call the Caribbean home. Under the umbrella with the Association of Bridal Consultants, this partnership with Sandals has given me the opportunity to complete training with Sandals as a Certified Sandals Specialist, CSS, and a Sandals Honeymoon Specialist, SHS. Mr. Gordon Stewart, and his son Adam Stewart, invited the ABC members to come to various locations throughout the Caribbean to stay at the resort for three or more days to experience their properties first hand. By doing so, we have firsthand experience of the property and can better convey that to our potential clients. Image waking up in the morning while lying in your king-sized four-poster bed looking directly at the blue and green water from your room, which is so close to the ocean you could touch it. You enjoy walking on the white sandy beach, with a tropical breeze, having your lunch on the beach and enjoying the evening entertainment daily on the property. You truly do not have to leave the property because they have a number of air, boat, water, golf, and spa activities for you to do all day. As for honeymoons and weddings, my guests are treated to the best suites possible for their honeymoon stay. They are first whisked away in a private transport from the airport directly to their room. Check-in is a breeze because we register our guests before they arrive so they do not have to wait and can get directly to their room and in the beautiful blue and green water. We arrange for private dining in their room, private dinner for two on the beach, and rose petals on the bed with sparkling cider or champagne depending on their taste. I love treating my honeymoon couples as well as families to the special treats. I always have repeat clients who go back repeatedly. Sandals provide us with a specialist at the client's property of choice for their wedding. We complete the layout, flowers, cake, and food for an interment group coming to the Caribbean for the wedding. The wedding is staged in the white sands on the beach at the property. Prior to all the final decisions the couple is invited down to the property for two days to review everything that has been put in place from room locations, to food, and where the ceremony will be held. From that point, the couple goes home with excitement and anticipation of the wedding and honeymoon to come. They cannot wait to share this beautiful experience with family and friends. The design part of the business is taking a room and transforming it into the vision of your client. My associations, in the industry of event and design planning, the classes, seminars, and live demonstrations have excited me and help me grow in this area. During an ABC Annual Conference, I got to see a presentation and meet Colin Cowie, who is a corporate member with ABC. Colin Cowie is an events expert whose business travels covers the four corners of the world doing everything from intimate birthday celebrations, iconic weddings, and corporate bashes. His love for design and business keeps him busy with all of his projects. Empowering people to live their best life and be the best person they can be is at the top of what motivates him to share his lust for life. After seeing his presentation and actually talking with him I have been inspired to design and transform event spaces for my clients. With the help of other like-mined associates, floral, linen, candles, and lighting, I have been able to work magic at event spaces for my clients. Each year our Association of Bridal Consultants, Maryland, and District of Columbia Chapter host a Winter State Educational Meeting. We have special guest speakers, updates on the ABC Annual Conference, Advancements of Designation within our Maryland Chapters, and Awards of Leadership. I was the first recipient of the Dezi Grant Scholarship in 2014, in which the recipient's expenses for the Annual Association of Bridal Consultant Conference are paid in full. At the Winter State Educational Meeting the Maryland, District of Columbia member register competed in a friendly competition among peers, which was a table design contest.

I enter the table design contest competition. This year February 2016 my design won second place in my category.

FEBRUARY 2016 TABLE DESIGN 2ND PLACE WINNER

The event business is an emotional journey, but you must not get so involved that you take it personal; you have a job to execute to make your client feel like a Queen or King for a Day! You are the one who was hired to get the job done. You must be skilled in proper communication and execute your timeline. Your timeline is your saving grace and lifeline. Your timelines assist in keeping your order of activities and events moving smoothly and therefore avoid problems. You cannot however, control the personality of people you might encounter. You have to think fast on your feet. Execute the wishes of your clients, ask the hard questions when no one else will, and sometimes you have to be all to all, as we say. You are responsible for all the duties as assigned when you are running a small business. At the end of the day, your clients will be pleased with how you had everything running like a well-oiled machine. To your clients, everything ran seamless. However, there were probably fires and drama that you and your team handled by extinguishing those fires and any concerns without the client knowing. You must always keep problems in the background and never bring them to the forefront. You must be able to address any guest issues and resolve them as quickly as possible. You must be tough-skinned and not take situations personal. It is not about you; it is about your client and their guests. You have to remove yourself from the emotions to get the job done, while staying personable and making sure your clients and guests are having a great experience.

I have learned that not all clients and jobs are for me. Some might think you should accept a paying job no matter what, but if the job does not fit you, your brand, or the image of your company, you may want to consider extending an offer to another associate to work the job, if possible.

Corporate events are very similar but different in that they have an established budget. They will assign an assistant to work with you to make sure the venue and events meet the needs of the corporate client. One of the most important items for corporate is the review aspect of your event, which is reviewed with additional sign offs for every step prior to the full approval. The set-up and design is paramount to determine the ease of audiovisual, lighting, microphones, stationary, lapel, and overhead are working properly. The layout of the stage is important, making sure there is enough space to move around while entering and exiting the stage. Extended meeting rooms and areas, which include food service, are worked in conjunction with the Catering Manager and the Banquet Officer. Upon meeting with them and reviewing the timeline of the Banquets Events Order (BEQ), everything should run smoothly. As you can visualize, there are many moving parts to acquiring and executing an event. It may be a wedding, honeymoon, or corporate event. All are similar, but the one thing which stays the same is the reputation that you have built that makes the client acknowledge that they have chosen your company to design and execute their event and they are impressed by you and your recommendations, which speak volumes in this industry. They want you to handle this for them because of your reputation, and trusting you to take care of the brand of their company. Clients will entertain using your services based on what they read, hear, and see. There is always room for improvement and I continue to learn and grow my company. I will always continue improving my skills to the next level for my business. I will always be evolving and moving at the speed of me!

Wedding Day, July 16, 2016, in Greenbelt Maryland

Mr. & Mrs. Paul & Diamond Quinichett, III.

CHAPTER 5

SO YOU THINK YOU WANT TO BE AN ENTREPRENEUR

So you think you want to be an entrepreneur. You have attended so many events, parties, baby showers, corporate meetings, weddings, graduations, and store openings. The list is never ending. There are many events to pick from. You sit in on your fifth baby shower, and it's not yours, you think to yourself, "If I see another blue or pink baby outfit and then have to act excited as if this was the first baby outfit I've seen, I am going to scream!" The decorations are the same, the games are the same, and didn't I see the same cake design just last month? You say to yourself, "I can do this. I can do a better job than what I see right now." Before you go out and buy yourself some business cards, stop and really think about what you would like to do. Think about your passion and what brings you joy. What is that business you cannot get out of your head? A business you fall asleep to dream about and wake up to. The excitement is so vivid and so real that you can image yourself in the business, running the business. You are the president of your company, and you are in charge! Now let's step back. After some soul searching, you have decided that you really would like to manage corporate meetings.

From the inside looking in, it seems easy. Being an event planner of any aspect is very detailed work. Start your research by asking questions of people you know whom is already doing corporate meeting planning. Listen to them, learn about what they have done, and determine how you can take some of these nuggets and incorporate them into your new and developing business. Each conversation you have with individuals in the event industry will lead you to another area that you may want to consider. Research classes, seminars, and open forums offered by banks, community civic centers, and government agencies. They all offer sessions on how to start a new business. You will find that the costs to take these seminars are small and sometimes free. Now that you have your area of interest picked out and a checklist of action items to put in place, you can begin your packet to begin setting up your business. Please remember that you need to register your business name, so again research the name you want to use. It took me over eight times to come up with a name. Of course, I had an ideal name, but it was already registered. You have to know that you are not the first person on the planet considering becoming an entrepreneur. In fact, the largest population of new entrepreneurs is women. To note just a few facts, thirty-six percent of all non-farm and non-publicly held businesses are owned by women. When broken down by race, women of color are more likely to own businesses than women overall; 59 percent of black-owned businesses are owned by women; 44 percent of Hispanic-owned businesses are owned by women; and 39 percent of Asian-owned businesses are owned by women. These percentages show that women are on the move when it comes to placing themselves in the business industry to be recognized. Businesses owned by women are increasing at much higher rates than their male counterparts. The number of women-owned businesses has increased nearly 3.5 times the rate of increase of men-owned businesses (68 percent and 19 percent respectively).

After you have looked at all the statics and determined what your business will be, identify who your target audience is, and what your global reach might be. Will you be able to do everything you need to implement to start and run a successful business? I learned the hard way. In the beginning of starting my business, I was the president; executive assistant, scheduler, accountant, and all around do all be all. I was a solo-preneur. You truly do need a village to help run your business. You will need to determine how you can bring on staff. I know you might think, "Staff? I am barely making enough money to pay for my supplies." However, you will need some help; you cannot do everything and be everywhere at once. An option would be to hire a student from a university who are training to be a Certified Meeting Planner (CMP). You can trade on-the-job training that they can use on their resume for part-time salary. I use novice members from the Association of Bridal Consultant, who are referred to me from our State Manager upon their initial training when they join ABC. Upon training with seasoned members, the novice members receive a written overview from us, which the novice member can use toward points to advance them to the next certification level. These students and beginning members can be used to pull in staff part-time to help you when needed. Always reach out to your industry for help, and you will always find help. You are almost ready to let the world know you exist. Step back and look at what you have done so far. What are the colors you will use for your business? Color is an important aspect for your business. We must consider what a potential client sees when they first look at our website. The color does not necessarily have to be bold or loud. However, your colors should be professional and convey your brand and image. Once you have established a social media platform, register your business with the most popular networking site for your business. This will help you gain global exposure. You never know where your next client will come from. However, you have to be prepared to accept the challenge and go. Establishing your business will take time, so do this process at your own speed. Also, know that you will modify and update your business many times, as you determine what you enjoy doing more compared to other aspects of your business. Do keep moving and growing with your business. Being an entrepreneur will be challenging, but know that these challenges will make you a better businessperson. You do not have to wait until everything is in place before you start working in your business. Just start. If you wait for everything to be perfect before you start, you will never get started. After all this and many more actions to put in place, you are now ready to start your first job. So, do you think you want to be an entrepreneur?

CHAPTER 6

CHECKLIST OF BUSINESS TIPS & STRATEGIES

- Research other businesses that are doing what you are considering.

- Consider your budget for getting your business up and running – items should include registration, license, and website/social media site/branding and design/home office or store front/training/travel/additional staff

- Find an organization you can join with like-minded people in the field you are considering. This will be paramount in helping you learn and grow.

- Acquire a mentor in your field that will be willing to let you shadow and learn from them. This would be an invaluable partnership.

- Determine your target audience – This will help you in the design of your business. Do not settle for your own zip code; think global.

- Consider your marketing plan- How you will let your target audience know who you are and how they can reach you.

- Your business should have a social presence – Today, clients use social media to connect with you more than any other media.

- Join or acquire registrations on partner sites to promote your business or other vendors associated within your field of business.

- Always be on time for every meeting with a potential client and business meeting. Arrive early.

- Follow-up to close all open conversations with a client or business vendor.

- Your attitude should be professional at all times. This speaks volumes and will go a long way with business relationships. Lead by example and have a good attitude.

- Always be available to lend a hand to fill any gaps- Sometimes the unexpected happens and you may need to move fast.

- Look your best at all times, even when you are not working. You never know when you will acquire a client.

- Be teachable. Always be open to learn. There is always room for growth.

CHAPTER 7

STEPS TO PLANNING A PHENOMINAL EVENT

1. Hire an event planner- a planner can help you navigate your event and assist you with your budget.

2. Determine a location where you would like to hold your event.

3. Determine your budget – by doing so, this will be your guiding principle for making a determination on other aspects.

4. Work with your event planner to assist you in finding a location that meets your needs.

5. Review and ask many questions regarding written agreements between you and the vendors you hire.

6. Hire vendors to assist in making your day what you envision it to be. Pay deposits and/or retainer fees by credit card for adequate tracking.

7. Construct a timeline of the details of your event to help manage and execute your plans.

8. Review any extra décor and special equipment

needed.

9. Review the banquet order with the catering manager for food service.

10. Confirm setup, arrival, and departure times for your vendors.

11. Review all aspects of your event with your event planner and confirm everything is in place.

12. Lights, Camera, Action, Go Time!

13. At the end, make sure all vendors have left the event space at the appropriate time and all equipment is removed.

CONCLUSION

What I have learned from writing this book is that education and being in the mindset to be teachable is key in business. My degree in business has helped me understand and navigate the many processes of how to interact with clients and the moving parts regarding the needs of clients and getting the job done. Working with children in the Washington Arts Program with the Department of Recreation program for inner city youth in Washington, D.C., where I grew up, opened my eyes to understanding that assistance is still, and will continue to be, needed to nurture our young people and show them a different life than the one they live. Education, growth, and mentorships with the Association of Bridal Consultants will always be my anchor which has guided me toward the new me! Growing up with so many siblings, many life lessons were observed and learned, which helped mold me. By taking a step to move you forward, doing something that scares you, challenges you, and makes you uncomfortable, is a growing experience. It is not worth the journey if it is easy; you should sweat for it. Moving at the speed of me is lethargic, in the sense that I know it is ok just to be me! I am moving at my own pace, not in a race. I am enough and I do not have to prove or win anyone's approval but my own. I challenge you to take your own journey and discover who you are and what your gifts are. Once you complete your discovery, go out and share you and your gifts with as many people as you can. Our lives will have no meaning if we do not leave a legacy. Always strive to do your best, moving at your speed. Your speed is the only thing that matters!

ABOUT THE AUTHOR

Olenthia R. Boardley is a seasoned professional event planner and is respected by her peers. Since 1997, Mrs. Boardley has completed numerous events and weddings. In addition, within the last six years she has arranged honeymoon travel plans for her guests. She is a Certified Wedding Planner (CWP) with The Association of Bridal Consultants (ABC), as well as a member of the Leadership Team and Co-Director for the Montgomery County Maryland Local Area Networking Group (LNG) for the Association of Bridal Consultants, Maryland/District of Columbia Chapter. She continues to learn, grow, and mentor new members as they join ABC by allowing them to shadow her and work on events with her company. By doing so, she is always giving back to her community and enhancing her love and excitement for the industry. She lives in Montgomery County, Maryland, with her family and leading a full life. Do not look at what other individuals are doing with their business and life; just run your own race at your speed and you will conquer. "Moving at the speed of me" is her mantra.

To learn more visit: www.orbsroyaltreatment.com

Email: info@orbsroyaltreatment.com